BOGIE & BACALL

Love Lessons from a Legendary Romance

CINDY DE LA HOZ

RUNNING PRESS
PHILADELPHIA • LONDON

To my funny Valentine

© 2015 by Cindy De La Hoz

Published by Running Press,
A Member of the Perseus Books Group
All rights reserved under the Pan-American and International Copyright Conventions

Printed in China

Books published by Running Press are available at special discounts for bulk purchases in the United States by corporations, institutions, and other organizations. For more information, please contact the Special Markets Department at the Perseus Books Group, 2300 Chestnut Street, Suite 200, Philadelphia, PA 19103, or call (800) 810-4145, ext. 5000, or e-mail special. markets@perseusbooks.com.

ISBN 978-0-7624-5796-0
Library of Congress Control Number: 2015946677
E-book ISBN 978-0-7624-5808-0

9 8 7 6 5 4 3 2 1
Digit on the right indicates the number of this printing

Designed by Ashley Haag
Edited by Jennifer Kasius
Typography: Neutra Text, Alex Brush, and Berling

Running Press Book Publishers
2300 Chestnut Street
Philadelphia, PA 19103-4371

Visit us on the web!
www.runningpress.com

INTRODUCTION

*H*umphrey Bogart was a man's man—not traditionally handsome by any measure, but he possessed a certain sex appeal that was made legendary in his role of the ultimate romantic hero in *Casablanca*. Lauren Bacall was a fledgling actress who had been enjoying a brief but fruitful career as a model, a stunning beauty who was twenty-five years Bogart's junior. While not outwardly a perfect pair, from the moment Bacall first appeared on the screen in *To Have and Have Not*, saucily asking Bogart for a light for her cigarette, their scenes together packed heat. No doubt about it, their chemistry was a match made in cinematic heaven.

Off-screen, their coupling as a romantic pair was less likely. By the time they met, Bogart—popularly known as Bogie—was a highly respected veteran of stage and screen, and had appeared in more than fifty films. He had also been married three times and his relationship with his current wife, Mayo Methot, was infamously tempestuous. The marriage was characterized by excessive drinking and headline-making volatility so much so that they were known as the "Battling Bogarts." Lauren—much better known by her given

name of Betty to anyone who knew her—was warned (only half-jokingly) that if Mayo's well-known jealousy surfaced she was likely to drop a lamp on Betty's head. It was quite a lot for an inexperienced nineteen-year-old to handle.

Betty Joan Perske, who had adopted Lauren Bacall as her screen name, had dreamed of acting professionally since childhood. She became an usherette on Broadway simply to place herself in close proximity to the theater world, entered drama school, and became a fashion model after *Harper's Bazaar* editor Nicolas de Gunzburg introduced her to Diana Vreeland, who put Betty on a now-legendary cover of the magazine. The wife of film producer Howard Hawks saw the cover and encouraged her husband to make a test of the green-eyed beauty. Hawks put Betty under a personal contract to him and decided to test her for his upcoming production, *To Have and Have Not*. Humphrey Bogart, the film's star, later told Betty, "I just saw your test. We're going to have a lot of fun together."

And they did have fun—from the first day of shooting when Bogie made jokes to calm his visibly nervous costar. A fast friendship turned into romance as Bogie and Betty soon found themselves falling hopelessly, desperately, and all consumingly in love with each other. Bogart had become resigned to life in an unhappy marriage. He saw in Betty the hope for a new future and she saw in him a "sentimental, loving, extraordinary man." She looked up to and admired him in a way she might have an actual father, which Betty had grown up without. She had never been in love before and was overwhelmed by the intense feelings growing between them. While becoming an actress had been her lifelong dream, she soon had no greater hope than for their future together. The goal was realized after Bogart and Mayo were divorced a year later.

Bogie and "Baby," as they were affectionately known to friends and each other, were married on May 21, 1945. By then *To Have and Have Not* had been released and Bacall had become the greatest new sensation in Hollywood—an "overnight" star. The next three years saw the release of three more hit Bogie and Bacall films in succession, *The Big Sleep*, *Dark Passage*, and *Key Largo*. As exciting as they were to watch together onscreen, in their private lives the couple's dynamic and devotion to each other was enviable even in Hollywood circles. Over the years they formed a tight circle of friends with fellow larger-than-life personalities such as Frank Sinatra, Judy Garland, David Niven, Spencer Tracy, and Katharine Hepburn. They had a son and daughter (Stephen and Leslie), shared passions in politics and hobbies, and professional success.

In 1956, their world was changed forever when Bogart became ill with what turned out to be esophageal cancer. He received the best care available and unfaltering support from Betty during his last few months of life, before passing away on January 14, 1957, at age fifty-seven. At thirty-two, Betty was a widow, but had no regrets. They seemed to pack a lifetime into twelve and a half years of marriage. She went on to great personal and professional successes over the course of the rest of her life, but cherished those years with Bogie. "Whenever I hear the word *happy* now, I think of then," said Bacall many years later. "Then I lived the full meaning of the word every day."

Bogie and Bacall overcame a world of obstacles and defied convention by having a marriage in Hollywood that really was till death do them part. For decades audiences have been looking up to them through their four unforgettable films on the big screen, but there is also endless inspiration to be found in their personal relationship. What follows are a few dozen ways Bogie and Bacall taught us all how to have a legendary romance.

DON'T SWEAR BY
"your type"

When young Betty Bacall first came to Hollywood,
her mentor, Howard Hawks, told her that he envisioned
her starring in a film with either Cary Grant or
Humphrey Bogart. The debonair Grant sounded much
more appealing to Betty at the time, but Hawks instead
made a screen test of her for Bogart's next film,
To Have and Have Not. She got the part and
never missed Mr. Grant.

GIVE A GUY
a second shot

Bacall was first introduced to Bogart on the set of his
film *Passage to Marseille* by Howard Hawks. "There
was no clap of thunder, no lightning bolt, just a simple
how-do-you-do." She thought he seemed nice, but
that spark of romantic interest didn't ignite until
midway through making their first film together.

TAKE *center* STAGE

By the time he made *To Have and Have Not* in 1943, Bogie was well on his way to becoming a movie legend. Bacall, only nineteen, hadn't a single film under her belt. Bogart did everything he could to put the newbie on set at ease and help her shine. Only Betty's nerves seemed to stand in her way. She began positioning her chin slightly downward to stop her nervous head from shaking. It became the signature Bacall look and her magnetism ignited the screen.

NURTURE EACH OTHER'S
hidden talents

Betty was going to be dubbed for the number she was due to sing in her first movie, Hoagy Carmichael's "How Little We Know," but at the last minute Bacall—bolstered by Bogie—worked up the courage to attempt the number herself. Contrary to rumors that she was dubbed, Bacall's own voice was on the film's soundtrack. The star would later show off the full force of her singing chops to thunderous success on Broadway.

Don't be afraid
TO MAKE
THE FIRST MOVE

On-screen Bacall was the aggressor. In *To Have and Have Not*, Slim (Betty) famously catches the attention of Steve (Bogie) by seductively lighting up a cigarette in front of him, and later teaching him how to whistle— "You just put your lips together, and blow."

GIVE *creatively*

Bogie gave Bacall a small gold whistle on a
charm bracelet with an inscription on it referencing
that immortal line from *To Have and Have Not*. It said,
"If you want anything, just whistle."

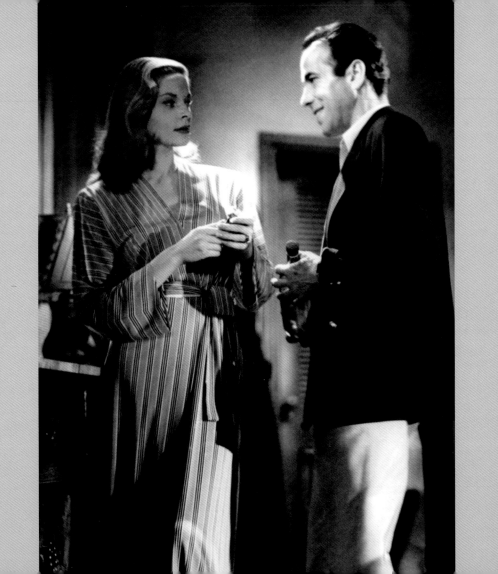

TURN "CORNY"
into cute

It's hard to believe when you see the sheer confidence she conveyed, but Betty's severe nerves were visible to all when they started working together. Bogart began telling her jokes in an effort to relax her. Though they were what Betty called "corny," those jokes did the trick, and so began an off-screen banter that was even more amusing than that heard on film.

TAKE HER
by surprise

At the end of a day's filming on their first movie
together, Bogart went to Bacall's dressing room
to say good-bye. He caught her off guard by
putting his hand to her chin and closing in for a
kiss. That was the start of their love affair.

Catch him
OFF GUARD

"Give her my love," Slim says to Steve when she hears
he's about to see Dolores Moran's character in *To Have
and Have Not*. "I'd give her my own if she was wearing
that dress," replies Steve. As a gag, Betty placed a small
photo of Bogie in the dress's center cutout and wore
it that way on set, to his utter amusement.

Remember
AGE IS
JUST A NUMBER

Bogart was forty-four when they met in 1943, Bacall barely nineteen. Her mother was against the relationship at first, partly due to their age difference, but that didn't dissuade Betty. Did she find Bogie to be old and tired in his mid-forties? On the contrary, she said "My challenge was to keep up with him. He was a man of extreme energy and intelligence."

DON'T *fight science*

Though it wasn't exactly love at first sight between Bogie and
Betty in real life, the camera picked up the electricity between
the couple immediately and projected it for the world to see.
That undeniable chemistry trumped the many barriers to their
romance. As Bacall once said, "You can't beat chemistry."

BE *passionate*

Betty described the beginning of their relationship as
"frantic, dangerous, romantic." He would call her in the middle
of the night, desperate to see his Baby. Years later director
John Huston casually asked Bogie and a few friends if any of
them would want to relive anything in their lives if they could.
Only Bogie spoke up: "When I was courting Betty."

INVENT *playful* NICKNAMES

At first they called each other Slim and Steve, after their characters' names in *To Have and Have Not*, then for a brief time Bogie nicknamed Betty "Harvey" after the hit play about a grown man with an imaginary friend—a giant rabbit named Harvey. That moniker was later bestowed on their boxer dog and "Baby" would be the nickname that stuck. It was Betty's officially, but both used the endearment with each other.

DON'T TAKE
YOUR PARTNER'S LOVE
for granted

"He adored me. I'd never had it before,
and I'll never have it again. I was lucky to have it at all."

—Lauren Bacall

KEEP YOUR
heart open

Betty's parents separated when she was very young, and
it caused the girl to be distrustful of love and marriage,
never believing that a relationship was meant to last.
Having anything less than the grand romance with
Bogie as her first love might have confirmed and forever
cemented those feelings that sprang from her parents'
split, but her heart remained open and let Bogie in.

TRUST YOUR
instincts

Everyone from Betty's mother to mentor Howard Hawks—
the people she trusted the most—told her she was making
a mistake getting involved with Bogie and that he was sure
to forget about her when their movie was finished. Decades
later Betty said that her romantic nature—and the naiveté
of her youth—could have completely steered her wrong, but
she seemed to know instinctively that Bogie truly loved her
and that this was only the start of their relationship.

TAKE AN
occasional gamble

Howard Hawks saw the makings of a great star in Betty—
one that he could relish in bolstering to the heights of the
Hollywood pantheon all by himself. Hawks had also become
infatuated with his protégé and was incensed that she went
and fell in love with Bogart. Her growing love outweighed the
risk of losing Hawks's professional support by marrying
Bogie, and she never regretted her decision.

Cultivate
SUPPORTIVE FRIENDS

Bogie so worried about the difference in their ages that he
lamented to his good friend, actor Peter Lorre, that there was
no way marriage to someone as young and beautiful as Betty,
just starting her career, could last more than five years. "Isn't five
years better than none?" said Lorre. Bogie concurred with his
friend's assessment and that helped convince him to marry Betty.

GET *lyrical*

Onscreen in *To Have and Have Not*, Steve tells Slim
he doesn't want any strings attached between them.
Off-screen Bogie waxed poetic. Riffing from Cole Porter's
then hit song, "Don't Fence Me In," he sent Betty a note
saying "Please fence me in, Baby—the world's too big out
here and I don't like it without you."

Find a perfect setting
FOR THOSE
special moments

On May 21, 1945, Bogie and Bacall were married.
Far from an elaborate affair amid Hollywood royalty, theirs
was a small ceremony with only close friends and family in
attendance, at the Ohio farm of author Louis Bromfield.

BE *sentimental*

After their wedding ceremony, the newly minted Mrs. Bogart
noticed tears running down her husband's face. When she
asked him why he was crying, Bogart said it was because
that was the first time he ever heard the words of the
ceremony and really felt their true meaning.

FOLLOW YOUR
heart's desire

At the start of their relationship, Bogie told Betty that each of his three previous wives were actresses, all of whom put their careers before their relationship and having a family. He did not want to go down that road again with Betty so he said he would help— though not marry—her if she wanted to devote herself to her career. While far from modern thought, for the duration of their marriage, Betty continued making movies but made family her top priority. She later said, "in view of the fact that we had such a short time together I'm damn glad that I did."

Join in on

EACH OTHER'S JOKES

The couple's back-and-forth crank call in *The Big Sleep* was one of the movie's highlights. Each topped the other line for line. While most of the movie was made before they were married, this scene needed to be reshot and was filmed after their May 1945 wedding, capturing the first onscreen interplay between the dynamic husband and wife.

Indulge
PET HOBBIES

Bacall called Bogie's boat, the *Santana*, her greatest
competition for her husband's attention. She didn't quite
share his passion for sailing but he helped her understand his
feeling for the sea, calling it the "last free place on earth."

MAKE
beautiful music
TOGETHER

Betty became famously associated with the piano after a headline-
making photo op in which Warner Bros. publicity chief Charlie
Enfield coaxed her into sitting atop Harry Truman's piano while the
then vice president played a tune. It was purely a publicity stunt
for the rising star at the time, but Betty was indeed very musically
inclined and sang onscreen and onstage for decades to come.

Toast
TOGETHER

Bogie once quipped "The problem with the world is
that everyone is a few drinks behind." He and Betty
loved hosting friends for cocktail hour. His favorite was
a classic martini. She loved a "milk punch" spiked with
bourbon, because she couldn't taste the bourbon.

Make friends
WITH THE IN-LAWS

At first Betty's mother strongly—and very vocally—objected to her daughter's romance with Bogart. In time she came to love him and they all became a tight-knit family, including Bogart's sister, Pat. Bogart served as best man at Betty's mother's marriage to Lee Goldberg. The ceremony was held at the Bogart residence.

KEEP
mementos

The cake topper from their wedding day remained
a sentimental keepsake throughout the Bogarts'
marriage and was brought out for anniversary
photos over the years.

Be silly
TOGETHER

One of the personality traits that first struck Betty about Bogie was his sense of humor. The nerdy affectation of upturned hat, glasses, and comic voice when he walks into the bookstore in *The Big Sleep* was Bogart's own idea to inject an impeccable dose of humor into the otherwise straight scene.

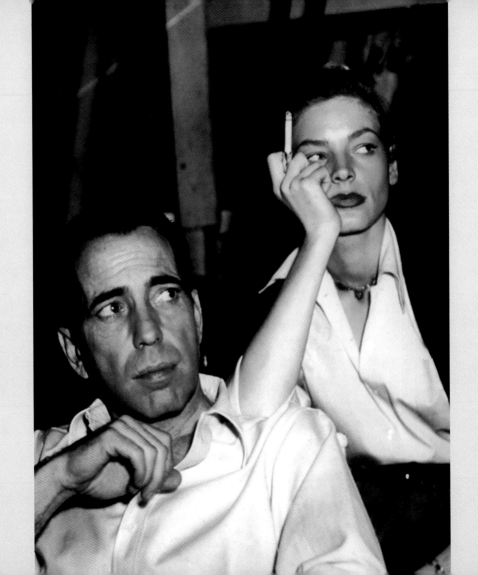

Be "boring"
TOGETHER

You know it's true love when you can simply
be contentedly quiet together.

HAVE THE
best repartee
IN TOWN

Bogie and Bacall could exchange witty lines of dialogue and double entendres like no other pair in Hollywood. The banter between them from their first shared moments onscreen would become legendary.

Love what you do—
AND DO IT TOGETHER
SOMETIMES

Both Bogart and Bacall loved the acting profession and took their work seriously. They also loved that it allowed them to work with so many actors, filmmakers, and crew whose work they deeply respected. But, of course, they cherished working with no one more than each other. They made four films together—*To Have and Have Not*, *The Big Sleep*, *Dark Passage*, and *Key Largo*.

Duke it out
TOGETHER

Onscreen Humphrey Bogart and Lauren Bacall were as
formidable as any famous crime-fighting duo. Cynical and
world-weary though they may have seemed, you knew
they were on the side of good and no one would outsmart
them in the end—except maybe each other.

NEVER *say* NEVER

In his mid-forties Bogie thought he'd never have
children, that his life was the way it was and would
remain so. It took a strong woman to change his mind.

PICK THE
perfect parent

Betty knew early on she wanted no one but Bogie as the
father of her children. She saw qualities in him—"integrity,
truth, and courage"—that she admired, aspired to, and
wanted to pass on to her kids. Having grown up without a
father herself, she hoped to give her own children a loving
father who would never let them feel abandoned.

Make room

FOR MORE

Although they'd planned on having children, when
Betty announced to Bogie that she was pregnant for
the first time, he became frightened that it wouldn't
be just the two of them anymore, that a child might
come between them. Of course it didn't, but only
brought an abundance of joy and love into their
home—a home that was expanded with the birth of
each child, at Betty's insistence.

Connect to
YOUR
BEGINNINGS

Born January 6, 1949, the Bogarts' first child was named Stephen, after the character Bogart played in the film that brought the couple together in 1944, *To Have and Have Not.*

RELISH THOSE
precious moments

They named their daughter, Leslie, after Bogie's one-time
mentor—and Betty's dream man as a young girl—Leslie Howard.
Betty loved to watch Bogart interact with their baby girl
because she said he regarded her with total awe,
a precious little girl.

SAIL *away*

Once Betty found her sea legs, climbing
aboard *Santana* and leaving their cares
behind on dry land became one of the couple's
most frequent and joyous pastimes.

Have a ball

Though they cherished family time alone, the
Bogarts were also among the best-loved hosts on
the Hollywood social scene. For them and friends,
Christmas Eve doubled as a celebration of Bogie's
birthday, and the couple's annual anniversary party
in May was an event not to be missed.

MAKE YOUR HOME
a sanctuary

Betty and Bogie moved a few times during their marriage,
primarily to accommodate their expanding family. With
care they made each house a home, complete with a
white-picket fence, but it was far from cliché; it was their
own haven and invitations to the Bogart residence were
a hot ticket in the film community.

Savor
THE SIMPLE MOMENTS

While the Bogarts loved entertaining and having their closest friends over for cocktails, they most treasured their time alone together at home. Evenings were often spent having dinner on trays and then watching television lounging on the couch.

Play
TOGETHER

Bogie was a first-class chess player and it was
one of the couples' favorite games.

HAVE A
canine mediator

Harvey was the Bogarts' beloved dog. Betty said he seemed more human than canine in his sensitivity. If he was present during an argument between Bogie and Betty, Harvey would pace from one to the other and growl, seemingly trying to make them stop fighting.

LET THE WORLD
fall away
SOMETIMES

"Always in the wee small hours when it seemed to Bogie and me that the world was ours—that we were the world. At those times we *were*."

—Lauren Bacall

BE *adventurous*

Betty joined Bogie and Katharine Hepburn for the filming of *The African Queen* deep in the jungles of the Congo, where the film production company had hired eighty-five natives to clear a camp for cast and crew. Enduring extreme heat, various infections and illnesses, and an occasional animal or insect invasion, the company made an extraordinary film—and the Bogarts cemented a close friendship with Katharine Hepburn.

Celebrate

EACH OTHER'S

triumphs

Bogart had always said he didn't believe in awards for acting—
that it wasn't a level playing field unless all actors were playing
the same part. When he was nominated for the Academy
Award as Best Actor for _The African Queen_, Bogie had a gag
speech in mind he said he would give if he happened to win.
But jokes were put aside when he actually won. Bogie was
touched by the recognition from his peers and said heartfelt
thank-yous upon accepting the award. No one was prouder
than Betty, beaming at him from the audience.

Support
EACH OTHER'S
causes

In the world in which the Bogarts moved, they had the opportunity to meet a great many esteemed individuals. Bacall wore her deep admiration and support of two-time Democratic presidential nominee Adlai Stevenson on her sleeve and she idolized him. Bogie indulged her "infatuation" with good humor and took up the campaign for Stevenson along with Betty.

BE A *cheerleader*

By her own choice, Bacall let her career take a backseat during their marriage, but Bogie never failed to champion her work. 1953's *How to Marry a Millionaire*, costarring Marilyn Monroe and Betty Grable, was a change of pace for Betty. She'd never starred in a comedy before. Bogart was proud to see the humor he loved about Betty shine on the screen and he cheered her on at the film's premiere alongside her glamorous costar.

LIVE LIFE
to the fullest

Bogie and Betty had all the best of life—a happy home, a son
and daughter, successful careers, and a tight circle of friends
and extended family—when Bogie suddenly fell ill. Though
he would be gone within months of being diagnosed with
esophageal cancer, Bogie and Betty savored every
last moment they had together.

Appreciate
WHAT'S WAITING FOR YOU AT HOME

When Bogie came home from an extended hospital stay
following surgery, he was greeted by the sight of Betty standing
at the top of the stairs with their children at either side of her,
waiting for him to come home. Bogie's reaction: "This is what it's
all about—this is why marriage is worth it."

Give praise

WHERE PRAISE IS DUE

Bogie encouraged Betty to make the film *Designing Woman* during the anxiety-filled time that he was ill. The movie was a comedy and a godsend for Betty under the circumstances to occupy her mind while enjoying working with her friend Gregory Peck. Bogart told Peck, "When the picture is over she comes home and takes care of me. That's how you separate the ladies from the broads."

Hold close
THE BEST OF FRIENDS

Katharine Hepburn and Spencer Tracy were among the
Bogarts' dearest friends. When Bogie was very ill near the end
of his life, Kate and Spencer visited nearly every night, and
were the couples' only friends welcomed into the bedroom
while Bogie rested. Betty asked Spencer to deliver her
husband's eulogy but he just couldn't bring himself to do it for
fear he'd fall apart saying good-bye to his friend.

Stick together
THROUGH
THICK *and* THIN

In his final months of life, Betty gave Bogie the utmost care with the help of nurses and kept his spirits up until the very end. After his passing, Betty buried him with that whistle he had given her before they were married.

LEARN *from her*

Though much older than his bride in 1945, Bogart found
he had a lot to learn from the young woman he had
fallen in love with. Among the many lessons were that it
was possible to be happily married, that they could have
mutual and supportive friends (there had been no love lost
between Bogie's previous wife and his friends), and that he
could still know what it was to love a child of their own.

Learn FROM HIM

"He changed me. He was my teacher, my husband, my friend. In his life and work, Bogie was integrity, truth, and courage. He taught me how to live, that it was okay to trust. He taught me to keep going, no matter what."

—*Lauren Bacall*

MARCH ON
in their stead

Bogart died on January 14, 1957, at age fifty-seven. Bacall would live for exactly fifty-seven more years. In those post-Bogie years, she experienced many of her greatest professional triumphs (including her childhood dream of conquering the Broadway stage) and raised children into adults their father would have been proud of. She lived a rich, fulfilling life, and—though she bristled at being called this during her lifetime—Lauren Bacall became a legend in her own right.

LEAVE A
legacy of love

In their twelve and a half years of marriage,
Bogie and Bacall became an iconic pair—an
inspiration to their contemporaries, idols to fans,
and the ultimate in true romance stories for
generations to come.

Photography Credits